THREATS TO CIVIL LIBERTIES

Threats to Civil Liberties:
PRIVACY

Bradley Steffens

San Diego, CA

About the Author

Bradley Steffens is a poet, a novelist, and an award-winning author of more than forty nonfiction books for children and young adults. He is a two-time recipient of the San Diego Book Award for Best Young Adult and Children's Nonfiction: his *Giants* won the 2005 award, and his *J.K. Rowling* claimed the 2007 prize. Steffens also received the Theodor S. Geisel Award for best book by a San Diego County author in 2007.

© 2019 ReferencePoint Press, Inc.
Printed in the United States

For more information, contact:
ReferencePoint Press, Inc.
PO Box 27779
San Diego, CA 92198
www.ReferencePointPress.com

LIBRARY OF CONGRESS CATALOGING-IN-PUBLICATION DATA

Name: Steffens, Bradley, 1955– author.
Title: Threats to Civil Liberties: Privacy/by Bradley Steffens.
Other titles: Privacy
Description: San Diego: ReferencePoint Press, Inc., [2019] | Series: Threats to Civil Liberties
Identifiers: LCCN 2018003240 (print) | LCCN 2018022227 (ebook) | ISBN 9781682824528 (eBook) | ISBN 9781682824511 (hardback)
Subjects: LCSH: Privacy, Right of—Juvenile literature. | Privacy—Juvenile literature.
Classification: LCC JC596 (ebook) | LCC JC596 .S737 2019 (print) | DDC 323.44/8—dc23
LC record available at https://lccn.loc.gov/2018003240

CONTENTS

The Right to Be Left Alone

The right to privacy has deep roots in American history— extending back to colonial times. According to John Adams, one of the founders of the United States and its second president, the right to privacy was a driving force behind the American Revolution. He recalled that in 1761 a patriot named James Otis gave a speech in Boston denouncing the British government's use of writs of assistance. These documents allowed British officers to enter the colonists' homes and search for evidence of criminal activity. The officers did not have to state why they were there or what they were looking for as they invaded the privacy of the homes. Letters, diaries, pamphlets—anything that seemed to associate the owner with crimes or revolutionary activities could be confiscated and used as evidence against the colonist. Adams later wrote, "Every man of a crowded audience appeared to me to go away, as I did, ready to take arms against writs of assistance." According to Adams, Otis's speech was "the first scene of the first act of opposition to the arbitrary claims of Great Britain. Then and there the child Independence was born."[1]

An Evolving Right

The concept of a right to privacy grew out of the idea of natural law. This was an Enlightenment-era concept that formed the basis of rights discussed in the Declaration of Independence, including the rights to life, liberty, and the pursuit of happiness.

These rights were considered universal—that is, they belonged to all people by birth, not as the result of any act by a king or government. The right to life included the right to not be physically injured. Gradually, protections against physical harm expanded to include protections against actions that create a condition of fear or anxiety. "In very early times, the law gave a remedy only for physical interference with life and property," wrote legal scholar Samuel D. Warren and future Supreme Court justice Louis D. Brandeis in 1890. "Gradually the scope of these legal rights broadened; and now the right to life has come to mean the right to enjoy life,—the right to be let alone."[2]

> "Gradually the scope of these legal rights broadened; and now the right to life has come to mean the right to enjoy life,—the right to be let alone."[2]
>
> —Samuel D. Warren and Louis D. Brandeis, legal scholars

Brandeis and others believed that then-emerging technologies such as snapshot photography and methods of sound recording posed a threat to the right to be left alone. "Instantaneous photographs and newspaper enterprise have invaded the sacred precincts of private and domestic life; and numerous mechanical devices threaten to make good the prediction that 'what is whispered in the closet shall be proclaimed from the house-tops,'"[3] wrote Warren and Brandeis.

Over time the right to privacy became recognized as a legal concept when courts interpreted existing laws and Congress and state legislatures passed new laws to protect individuals from such technological invasions. These laws forbade taking photographs, movies, and videos without permission; listening to and recording private conversations with hidden microphones; and eavesdropping on private phone conversations via wiretaps. Law enforcement, the press, businesses, and even individuals all faced criminal or civil penalties for invading a person's privacy. These safeguards were not perfect, but they prevented many abuses and gave people the right to recover damages in civil courts if their privacy rights were violated.

John Adams (pictured), one of the founders of the United States and its second president, said that the right to privacy was a driving force behind the American Revolution.

A Growing Challenge

The advent of the Internet and the proliferation of cell phones equipped with cameras have put new pressures on these restraints. Technologies are evolving so fast and their use is so pervasive that existing laws and social restraints are failing to protect individual privacy. Countless surveillance cameras and sensors in the interconnected network of devices known as the Internet of Things record the activities of people as they go about their daily business in public and even at home. Law enforcement agencies monitor cell phone activity, looking for criminal and terrorist activity. Corporations process vast amounts of data about both online and brick-and-mortar shoppers, searching for ways to increase sales and profits. Criminals with advanced computing skills access private information stored on computers—from tax returns to medical records—to steal identities to commit fraud or to demand ransoms for stolen data.

Meanwhile, social media providers compile vast storehouses of information about billions of persons' identities, including not only names, addresses, and phone numbers but also the names of friends, family members, and organizations they associate with as well as their images and their likes, dislikes, and buying habits. "A service like IBM's Personality Insights can build a detailed profile of you, moving well beyond basic demographics or location information," writes Jungwoo Ryoo, an associate professor of information sciences and technology at Pennsylvania State University. "Your online habits can reveal aspects of your personality, such as whether you are outgoing, environmentally conscious, politically conservative, or enjoy travel in Africa."[4]

> **"Privacy is the foundation of all other rights."[5]**
>
> —Edward Snowden, privacy advocate

The Foundation of All Rights

The vast amount of data being gathered about every person living in the digital society presents the potential for countless invasions of privacy. "Privacy isn't about something to hide, privacy is about something to protect. It is about protecting our rights, it is about protecting a free and open society," government whistle-blower and privacy advocate Edward Snowden told an Australian audience in 2016. "Privacy is the foundation of all other rights, privacy is the ability to make mistakes without prejudice and judgement as long as they are harmless. As long as a court or judge doesn't say, 'we have evidence this person is a criminal, you need to start watching them,' you are presumed to be left alone."[5]

CHAPTER 1

Government Spying

In April 2011, police in Detroit, Michigan, arrested four men suspected of committing a series of armed robberies at Radio Shacks and T-Mobile stores in the area. Hoping for leniency, one of the suspects confessed his guilt. He told police that he and the other three men had robbed nine different stores in Michigan and Ohio between December 2010 and March 2011, working with a group of accomplices and led by a man named Timothy Carpenter. Because the robbers had crossed state lines, the robberies became federal crimes, and the Federal Bureau of Investigation (FBI) took over the investigation.

The robber who confessed gave the FBI his cell phone number and the numbers of his accomplices. In May and June 2011, the FBI received three orders from judges allowing it to obtain calling records from the wireless carriers for the suspects' phone numbers. These records contained details such as the numbers called, the time of day the calls were made, and the service areas of the cell phone towers that handled the calls. The time and location information helped the FBI establish the movements of the suspects and tie them to the crimes.

At trial, Timothy Carpenter's lawyers argued that the cell phone records could not be used as evidence against him because using them violated the US Constitution's protections of personal privacy. The judge dismissed the claim, and Carpenter and others were found guilty. Carpenter was sentenced to 116 years in prison. His lawyers appealed the case to the US Supreme Court, which heard arguments in November 2017.

The Fourth Amendment

At issue in *Carpenter v. United States* is the meaning of the Fourth Amendment to the US Constitution. It states,

> The right of the people to be secure in their persons, houses, papers, and effects, against unreasonable searches and seizures, shall not be violated, and no warrants shall issue, but upon probable cause, supported by oath or affirmation, and particularly describing the place to be searched, and the persons or things to be seized.

The wording of the Fourth Amendment grew out of the founders' experience with writs of assistance and the sweeping searches they permitted. Under the Fourth Amendment, law enforcement authorities must describe to a judge the specific crime they believe has been committed—the probable cause—before they can obtain a search warrant. They also must specify what type of evidence they expect to find. The amendment mentions *persons*, *houses*, *papers*, and *effects*, but these terms are broad enough to cover many things. This includes apartments, houseboats, and motorhomes—not just houses. It includes photographs, tape recordings, and computer files—not just papers. It includes every kind of effect imaginable, from jewelry boxes to automobiles. The US Supreme Court, which interprets the meaning of the Constitution, has applied the Fourth Amendment to the modern government methods of gathering evidence that can invade a person's privacy. This includes the ability of law enforcement authorities to listen in on phone conversations, known as wiretapping; to eavesdrop on conversations using small electronic microphones and transmitters, known as bugs; and to intercept electronic communications such as text messages and e-mails. The question before the court in *Carpenter* was whether or not a person's cell phone records fall under the protections of the Fourth Amendment.

When the issue of intercepting electronic communications first came up, the majority of the Supreme Court justices saw no problem with listening in on a conversation, provided the law enforcement agents did not trespass into a person's home. In a case known as *Olmstead v. United States* (1928), federal agents had wiretapped telephone calls made by a bootlegger named Roy Olmstead. Olmstead's attorneys argued that the wiretaps violated their client's Fourth Amendment rights, but the high court upheld the conviction. It reasoned that wiretaps were permissible because the federal agents had not invaded Olmstead's house nor any of his physical property.

In order for law enforcement authorities to search private cell phone records such as texts and e-mails, the Fourth Amendment requires investigators to first obtain permission from a judge.

Safeguarding Phone Conversations

Thirty-nine years after *Olmstead*, the high court reversed itself. In two cases, *Katz v. United States* (1967) and *Berger v. New York* (1967), the court ruled that law enforcement officers needed search warrants in order to listen in on phone conversations and to record conversations using hidden listening devices. "Few threats to liberty exist which are greater than that posed by the use of eavesdropping devices," stated the court in *Berger*. "It is not asking too much that officers be required to comply with the basic command of the Fourth Amendment before the innermost secrets of one's home or office are invaded."[6]

In *Katz*, the Supreme Court extended the Fourth Amendment's protections beyond the walls of a person's home to any situation where a person has a reasonable expectation of privacy. "The Fourth Amendment protects people, not places," wrote Justice Potter Stewart for the majority. "What a person knowingly exposes to the public, even in his own home or office, is not a subject of Fourth Amendment protection. But what he seeks to preserve as private, even in an area accessible to the public, may be constitutionally protected."[7] Federal agents had placed listening devices on the outside of a public telephone booth from which Charles Katz had placed bets by phone in violation of interstate gambling laws. When Katz closed the door to the telephone booth, the court held, he had a reasonable expectation of privacy. A reasonable expectation, the court said, is an expectation that is both held by an individual and is considered reasonable by society.

In Carpenter's case, the police did not listen in on any conversations. The investigators only used information the cell phone providers had saved about when and where Carpenter's cell phone had contacted the local wireless antennas, known as cell

> "The Fourth Amendment protects people, not places. What a person . . . seeks to preserve as private, even in an area accessible to the public, may be constitutionally protected."[7]
>
> —Justice Potter Stewart of the US Supreme Court

Phone Records Are Private

Justice Potter Stewart wrote a dissenting opinion to the Supreme Court's decision in *Smith v. Maryland* (1979). In it, he argues that the telephone numbers a person dials are private information and are therefore protected by the Fourth Amendment. Below is an excerpt of that opinion.

> A telephone call simply cannot be made without the use of telephone company property and without payment to the company for the service. . . . Yet we have squarely held that the user of even a public telephone is entitled "to assume that the words he utters into the mouthpiece will not be broadcast to the world."
>
> The numbers dialed from a private telephone—although certainly more prosaic than the conversation itself—are not without "content." Most private telephone subscribers may have their own numbers listed in a publicly distributed directory, but I doubt there are any who would be happy to have broadcast to the world a list of the local or long distance numbers they have called. This is not because such a list might in some sense be incriminating, but because it easily could reveal the identities of the persons and the places called, and thus reveal the most intimate details of a person's life.

Quoted in Justia, "*Smith v. Maryland*, 442 U.S. 735 (1979)." https://supreme.justia.com.

phone towers. Obtaining this information was similar, lawyers for the government said, to a 1979 case, *Smith v. Maryland*, in which the Supreme Court held that the police did not need a warrant to track numbers a person dialed from a home phone because the caller could not have a reasonable expectation of privacy. "All telephone users realize that they must 'convey' phone numbers to the telephone company, since it is through telephone company switching equipment that their calls are completed," wrote Justice Harry Blackmun for the majority in *Smith*. "We doubt that people in general entertain any actual expectation of privacy in the num-

Phone Records Are Not Private

Justice Harry Blackmun wrote the Supreme Court's majority opinion in *Smith v. Maryland*. In this excerpt, Blackmun explains why phone records are not protected by the Fourth Amendment.

> Even if petitioner did harbor some subjective expectation that the phone numbers he dialed would remain private, this expectation is not "one that society is prepared to recognize as reasonable." This Court consistently has held that a person has no legitimate expectation of privacy in information he voluntarily turns over to third parties. . . .
>
> When he used his phone, petitioner voluntarily conveyed numerical information to the telephone company and "exposed" that information to its equipment in the ordinary course of business. In so doing, petitioner assumed the risk that the company would reveal to police the numbers he dialed. The switching equipment that processed those numbers is merely the modern counterpart of the operator who, in an earlier day, personally completed calls for the subscriber. . . .
>
> We therefore conclude that petitioner in all probability entertained no actual expectation of privacy in the phone numbers he dialed, and that, even if he did, his expectation was not "legitimate."

Quoted in Justia, "*Smith v. Maryland*, 442 U.S. 735 (1979)." https://supreme.justia.com.

bers they dial." As a result, the court decided, the government's collection of numbers that were dialed "was not a 'search,' and no warrant was required."[8]

A Changing Technological Landscape

Attorneys for Carpenter said the technology at issue in their case was different from that in *Smith* and another case, *United States v. Miller* (1976), which was concerned with the government obtaining incriminating records from financial institutions.

"I think it's important to remember that *Miller* and *Smith* were decided four decades ago," Nathan F. Wessler, the attorney for Carpenter, told the high court during oral arguments. "The Court could not have imagined the technological landscape today."[9]

> "The collection of [cell phone location] information is a search, as it disturbs people's long-standing, practical expectation that their longer-term movements in public and private spaces will remain private."[10]
>
> —Attorney Nathan F. Wessler

Wessler argued that the difference between his client's case and *Smith* was that the government used the cell phone records like "a kind of time machine" to go back and track his client's movements over an extended period of time— 127 days. "The collection of this information is a search, as it disturbs people's long-standing, practical expectation that their longer-term movements in public and private spaces will remain private."[10] The facts of Carpenter's case, Wessler argued, more closely resembled those in *United States v. Jones* (2012). In that case, the court found that the government's tracking of a person's movements over hundreds of days by placing a GPS device on the exterior of a vehicle was a search under the Fourth Amendment and thus required a warrant.

The Third-Party Doctrine

Michael R. Dreeben, the attorney arguing on behalf of the government, said that Carpenter's case was completely different from *Jones* because the police did not invade Carpenter's car or any of his personal property to obtain information about his movements. Instead, the police went to a third party (the cell service provider), just as happened in the *Smith* case. "The technology here is new, but the legal principles that this Court has articulated under the Fourth Amendment are not. The cell phone companies in this case function essentially as witnesses being asked to produce business records of their own transactions with customers,"[11] Dreeben told the court.

Dreeben observed that when people use their cell phone service, they necessarily communicate with the service provider. It is reasonable, Dreeben said, to assume that cell phone users know the information is not private. Justice Anthony Kennedy seemed to agree. "It seems to me there's a much more normal expectation that businesses have your cell phone data. I think everybody, almost everybody, knows that," Kennedy said from the bench. "If I know it, everybody does,"[12] Kennedy added, making fun of his own limited knowledge of communications technology.

When the government asks the cell phone providers to produce these records, Dreeben argued, "it is doing the same thing that it did in *Smith*. It is doing the same thing that it did in *Miller*. It is asking a business to provide information about the business's own transactions with a customer. And under the third-party doctrine, that does not implicate the Fourth Amendment rights of the customer."[13]

The Privacy of E-Mail

As the discussions in *Jones* and *Carpenter* show, Congress and the Supreme Court have been trying to define privacy rights in the digital age. In 1986 Congress extended Fourth Amendment protections to e-mail by passing the Electronic Communications Privacy Act. Under this law, the government needs a search warrant to intercept e-mails or to read them once they have been stored on a person's personal computer or phone. E-mails stored on a remote e-mail server—such as those operated by Microsoft, Yahoo, Google, and others—are treated differently, however. If e-mails have not been opened, and have been on the remote servers for 180 days or less, law enforcement officers need a search warrant to view the contents. However, if e-mails have been opened and are left on the third-party computers, the government can access them with a lesser court order or a subpoena from a grand jury.

To obtain these types of court orders, the law enforcement agency does not need to show that the e-mails are likely to contain evidence of a crime, meeting the probable cause standard

Opened e-mails that are left on third-party e-mail servers, such as those operated by Google for Gmail, can be accessed by the government without a search warrant. All that is needed is a lesser court order or a subpoena.

required by the Fourth Amendment. Instead, the government only needs to show that the e-mails may contain evidence of criminal activity—a lower standard. The thinking here is that a person who has opened an e-mail and left it on a third-party server does not have the same expectation of privacy as someone who has down-loaded an e-mail to a computer. An e-mail on a remote server that has not been opened for more than 180 days can be searched with the lesser court orders as well. The logic there is that an e-mail that has not been read in approximately six months is of lesser im-portance to the e-mail account holder than a newer one would be.

The Need for an Update

Many organizations interested in privacy rights believe the Elec-tronic Communications Privacy Act's protections are inadequate.

"Thomas Jefferson knew the letters he stored in his office at Monticello would remain private," states the American Civil Liberties Union (ACLU), a nonprofit organization that defends individual rights. "Today's citizens deserve no less protection just because their 'papers and effects' might be stored electronically. Unfortunately, the main law governing the privacy of electronic communication—the Electronic Communications Privacy Act (ECPA)—was written in 1986, three years before the Web was even invented, and it is in sore need of an update."[14]

The shortcomings of the ECPA's rules about e-mail privacy are also on display in a case argued before the Supreme Court in February 2018—*United States v. Microsoft Corporation*. In this case, the government presented Microsoft with a warrant to search the e-mails of a person being investigated for illegal drug trafficking. Microsoft refused to comply, stating that the e-mails in question are not stored on servers in the United States but rather on servers located in Dublin, Ireland, and thus are beyond the reach of a US search warrant. "When Congress enacted the Stored Communications Act (SCA) in 1986, it said absolutely nothing about applying the Act to reach communications stored overseas," wrote Microsoft in a brief submitted to the US Supreme Court. "Congress did not focus on—and could scarcely have imagined—a world where a technician in Redmond, Washington, could access a customer's private e-mails stored clear across the globe. Yet the Government asks this Court to extend the SCA to private e-mails stored in Ireland. The Government is in the wrong forum."[15]

The government, however, contends that since the crimes in question were committed in the United States, the e-mails are subject to American search warrants, as the Supreme Court has ruled in earlier cases. As circuit judge Reena Raggi pointed out when she heard the Microsoft case in the lower court, Microsoft's interpretation of the law would allow it to ignore search warrants simply by moving the electronic files to computers located overseas. On the other hand, privacy experts worry that upholding the search warrant could lead to a massive invasion of privacy. "If U.S. law enforcement can obtain the e-mails of foreigners stored outside the United States, what's to stop the government of another country from getting your e-mails even though they are located in the United States?"[16] wrote Brad Smith, Microsoft's president and chief legal officer.

Intercepting E-Mails

The privacy of global communications also surfaced as an issue when former government employee Edward Snowden revealed secret documents he had taken from the National Security Agency (NSA), which is responsible for collecting and processing data for intelligence purposes. The documents showed that the NSA routinely captures and reads e-mails sent from the United States to people overseas. The NSA was given the authority to intercept foreign e-mails by Congress in 2008 with amendments to the Foreign Intelligence Surveillance Act (FISA) that were designed to fight terrorism. The NSA says that it focuses its efforts on about one hundred thousand terrorism targets overseas. However, 90 percent of the 160,000 intercepted documents Snowden gave to the *Washington Post* were not sent to or from targets at all but were incidental messages swept up by NSA procedures. Half of the documents contained names, e-mail addresses, or other details that the NSA marked as belonging to US citizens or residents.

> "The Fourth Amendment as it was written—no longer exists. Now we have a system of pervasive pre-criminal surveillance."[18]
>
> —Edward Snowden, a whistle-blower and privacy advocate

The NSA program did lead to the 2011 capture in Abbottabad of Muhammad Tahir Shahzad, a terrorist bomb builder based in Pakistan, and Umar Patek, a suspect in a 2002 terrorist bombing on the Indonesian island of Bali. However, the e-mails given to the *Washington Post*, the newspaper reported, contained "stories of love and heartbreak, illicit sexual liaisons, mental-health

In 2008 the NSA was given the authority by Congress to intercept foreign emails. This program led to the 2011 capture of Umar Patek (pictured), a suspect in a 2002 terrorist bombing in Indonesia.

crises, political and religious conversions, financial anxieties and disappointed hopes."[17] This was exactly the kind of thing the Fourth Amendment was designed to prevent, according to Snowden. "The Fourth Amendment as it was written—no longer exists," writes Snowden. "Now we have a system of pervasive pre-criminal surveillance, where the government wants to watch what you're doing just to see what you're up to, to see what you're thinking even behind closed doors."[18]

Rajesh De, an attorney with the NSA, believes that concerns about government surveillance are greatly exaggerated. In a speech to the Georgetown University Law School in 2013, De outlined "three pervasive false myths about NSA." These include that the NSA "indiscriminately sweeps up and stores global communications," that it spies "on Americans at home and abroad with questionable or no legal basis," and that it "operates in the shadows free from external scrutiny or any true accountability."

He suggested that the information leaked by Snowden offered nothing more than a snapshot of what is in fact a continuous process of handling information about Americans. "To the extent that information to, from, or about U.S. persons is acquired incidentally as part of NSA's foreign intelligence mission, there are . . . rules in place to address the collection, handling, use, and destruction of such information consistent with the Fourth Amendment."[19] Information such as the love stories and other personal data highlighted by the *Washington Post* is not stored forever but rather is destroyed once it is determined to be of no value, De said.

Warrantless Surveillance

At the same time the NSA was monitoring e-mails, it also was intercepting phone calls and text messages to and from people outside the United States, again without search warrants. In 2010 the *Washington Post* reported, "Every day, collection systems at the National Security Agency intercept and store 1.7 billion e-mails, phone calls and other types of communications."[20] In the vast majority of these cases, the NSA was not actually listening to the phone conversations. As in the *Carpenter* case, the NSA investigators were mainly examining information about the calls and texts, known as metadata. This information includes the phone numbers, locations, times, and dates of the communications. The NSA used computers to analyze the bulk phone surveillance, searching for patterns that might reveal terrorist activities.

In January 2006 the ACLU sued the NSA to stop the warrantless surveillance program. The ACLU prevailed in the first hearing in August 2006. US District Court judge Anna Diggs Taylor found that the NSA program violated FISA and the Fourth Amendment's protections against warrantless searches. "It was never the intent of the Framers to give the President such unfettered control, particularly where his actions blatantly disregard the parameters clearly enumerated in the Bill of Rights,"[21] wrote Taylor in her forty-three-page decision.

The NSA appealed, and in 2007 the Sixth Circuit Court of Appeals dismissed the lawsuit. The court ruled that the ACLU and other parties to the suit had no standing, meaning they had not been targeted or harmed by the NSA's actions and therefore had no grounds for a lawsuit. Because of this, the judges did not consider the merits of the case itself. The ACLU appealed the ruling to the US Supreme Court in October 2007, but the high court declined to hear the case.

More lawsuits followed, and some are still pending. However, in 2015 Congress ended the warrantless wiretap program when it passed the USA Freedom Act. The law forbids the NSA from collecting phone metadata unless it has a warrant from the court set up by FISA to investigate terrorism. In November 2015 the NSA ended its bulk phone surveillance program. However, the agency continues to collect e-mails, texts, phone calls, and other private communications of foreigners abroad from American companies, such as AT&T, Google, and Yahoo. In January 2018 Congress renewed a controversial portion of the FISA Amendments Act known as Section 702, which permits the warrantless collection of data related to foreign intelligence operations from third parties. "We need our armed forces and intelligence community to protect us, and they need us to give them the tools to do it,"[22] said Senate majority leader Mitch McConnell after the vote.

Senator Ron Wyden of Oregon was disappointed that Congress did not amend the law to provide greater privacy protections. He said that failing to make changes in the law was "a dereliction of duty by a Congress that has a responsibility to protect Americans' freedoms, as well as our country's security." Congress authorized Section 702 for another six years, but Wyden promised to keep working "to protect Americans from unnecessary government spying."[23]

CHAPTER 2

Corporate Prying

Some laws passed by Congress, such as the Communications Act of 1934, are designed to prevent invasions of privacy not only by the government but also by individuals and companies. However, if a business notifies a customer that it might collect information about that person in the process of performing a service, and the person agrees to it, then that company is permitted to gather such data. For example, people who use social networking websites agree to terms of service that allow the social networking company to use their data. The same is true for the smartphone apps and search engines they use, the websites they visit, the financial transactions they perform, and many other types of data they generate as they go about their daily lives. None of these bits of information seem very important by themselves, but when all the pieces are put together, the companies gathering the data can create a detailed profile of a person's interests, activities, likes, and dislikes. This kind of profiling threatens privacy in ways that have never been used—or that have never even existed—before.

Big Data Analytics

The profiling of people using digital data is not done by human beings but rather by computers programmed with custom algorithms, or instructions, designed to find meaning in the seemingly random things people do. Many of these algorithms use a technique known as big data analysis to immediately process the actions people take online.

Big data is often described using four words beginning with the letter *v*: volume, velocity, variety, and veracity. Big data consists of large amounts of digital data (volume) that is generated at high speed (velocity). It is made up of many kinds of information (variety) and comes from sources that may or may not be known or trusted (veracity). For example, the 319 million active users of the social media platform Twitter post a large volume of data every day—more than 500 million tweets. This data is generated at a high velocity—at a rate of about 6,000 tweets every second on average. The tweets consist of a variety of content: text, numerals, emojis, pictures, and even short videos. Some of the people posting may be using fictitious names and posting false information. Big data programs process the large volume of data quickly, analyze all types of data, and apply "trust" rules to limit the impact of phony data. As a result, big data programs can find meaningful patterns in the data to make accurate predictions or draw intelligent conclusions. For example, big data analysts Tom Jackson and Martin Sykora at Loughborough University in the United Kingdom correctly predicted the election of Donald Trump in 2016 using their analysis of millions of tweets, even while traditional opinion polls were predicting an easy win for Trump's opponent, Hillary Clinton. "In the three weeks ahead of November 8, our model was telling us Trump was ahead based on the measures we were using,"[24] says Sykora.

Fraud Prevention

Big data technologies are employed by financial institutions to prevent fraud. Most people use bank cards or credit cards to pay for purchases big and small, every day. These transactions are transmitted electronically to the financial service provider, such as a bank, which maintains digital records of the transactions. Financial services companies use big data analytics to watch for suspicious activity, such as a series of large purchases in a short period. The computerized systems also compare current transactions to past

Big data analysts can find meaningful patterns in large quantities of information that can accurately predict trends. For example, based on a study of millions of tweets, two British analysts correctly predicted Donald Trump would beat Hillary Clinton in the 2016 presidential election.

transactions to see whether there are unusual changes, such as in the card user's location. If purchases are made in a city far from the user's home address, for example, the transactions might be flagged by the computer. The fraud prevention system will often send notices—e-mails or text messages—to the cardholder to verify that he or she actually made the purchases. If the cardholder did not make the purchases, the computer system can act instantly to block further use of the card.

Big data systems are able to make sense of financial activities in ways that older data processing systems could not. For example, if a customer uses a bank card to pay for an airline ticket and hotel reservation, the system uses such information, known as a data point, when looking for fraud. If a customer books a trip to Paris for a certain period of time and then uses a bank card there during that time, the system will not consider that suspicious, even though the purchase is made far from the user's home address. The system can correlate the location of the transaction to the information about the hotel reservation to determine that the purchase is probably not fraudulent.

Many fraud detection systems use the process of machine learning to evaluate information. Financial services company American Express told *Forbes* magazine in 2016 that its machine learning system is capable of evaluating thousands of data points on each transaction in less than two milliseconds. This high-speed analysis is used to evaluate the fraud risk on $1 trillion in charges across the American Express network each year.

Most people welcome the fraud protection that big data analytics provide, but others worry about how much data the financial services companies acquire regarding a person's activities. In his dissent to *United States v. Miller*—the 1976 Supreme Court case that allowed the government to access citizens' bank records without a search warrant—Justice William Brennan described the sensitive nature of the information a person shares with his or her bank.

"In the course of such dealings, a depositor reveals many aspects of his personal affairs, opinions, habits, and associations. Indeed, the totality of bank records provides a virtual current biography,"[25] wrote Brennan. The information is so confidential that Brennan believed the bank customer has a reasonable expectation of privacy, which would require the government to obtain a search warrant to search his or her records.

> "The totality of bank records provides a virtual current biography."[25]
>
> —US Supreme Court justice William Brennan

When Brennan expressed his views, bank records consisted mainly of a list of checks the customer had written. Checks usually bore only the date and the name of the person or entity to whom the funds were to be given, known as the payee. With today's bank cards, credit cards, and mobile payment systems such as Apple Pay and Samsung Pay, financial institutions obtain not only the name of the payee and the date of a transaction but also the time of day the payment was made, the location of the transaction, and what the payment was for. As US Supreme Court justice Samuel Alito Jr. observed during oral arguments in

Algorithmic Decisions Threaten Privacy

The Electronic Privacy Information Center is a nonprofit organization with the mission of focusing public attention on emerging privacy and civil liberties issues. It believes that using algorithms to make decisions about consumers without disclosing the factors that form the basis for decisions is a threat to privacy:

> Algorithms are complex mathematical formulas and procedures implemented into computers that process information and solve tasks. Advancements in artificial intelligence (AI), machines capable of intelligent behavior, are the result of integrating computer algorithms into AI systems enabling the system to not only follow instructions but also to learn.
>
> As more decisions become automated and processed by algorithms, these processes become more opaque and less accountable. The public has a right to know the data processes that impact their lives so they can correct errors and contest decisions made by algorithms. Personal data collected from our social connections and online activities are used by the government and companies to make determinations about our ability to fly, obtain a job, get security clearance, and even determine the severity of criminal sentencing. These opaque, automated decision-making processes bear risks of secret profiling and discrimination as well as undermine our privacy and freedom of association.

Electronic Privacy Information Center, "Algorithmic Transparency: End Secret Profiling." https://epic.org.

Carpenter v. United States, a modern bank record will show "everything that the person buys, it will not only disclose locations, but it will disclose things that can be very sensitive."[26]

Abuses of Credit Histories

Businesses have a keen interest in the details about a person's financial life—an interest that can intrude deeply into

Algorithmic Decisions Do Not Threaten Privacy

Jonathan H. King is head of portfolio management for Ericsson, a multi-national networking and telecommunications company headquartered in Stockholm, Sweden. He does not see algorithmic decisions as a threat to privacy:

> Much of the confusion about privacy law over the past few decades has come from the simplistic idea that privacy is a binary, on-or-off state, and that once information is shared and consent given, it can no longer be protected. These binary notions of privacy are particularly dangerous today and erode trust in our era of big data and metadata, in which private information is necessarily shared to some extent in order to be useful. . . .
>
> If I tell you my secret, the idea doesn't stop being a secret. Odds are that if I am telling you a secret, then there is some kind of informal or formal trust relationship between us. . . . Privacy is not merely about keeping secrets, but about the rules we use to regulate information. Privacy rules are information rules, and in an information society, information rules are inevitable. When properly understood, privacy rules will be an essential and valuable part of our digital future—a future not ordained to take a single, shiny, privacy-denying form but, instead, a human creation.

Jonathan H. King, "Here's Why Big Data Will Not Destroy Privacy," *Ericsson Future Digital Blog*, March 30, 2016. http://cloudblog.ericsson.com.

a person's privacy. Companies known as credit bureaus use details about a person's payment history, salary, occupation, employer, employment history, and other information from a variety of sources to determine whether or not a person is likely to pay back a loan in full. Lenders, including banks, credit card companies, and even car dealerships, obtain these credit ratings to make decisions about whether or not to offer a person a loan.

Evaluating a person's credit risk is a legitimate business use of financial information, but some privacy experts object to using credit reports and other algorithms to make decisions that affect a person's future, including decisions regarding hiring and college admissions and even the sentencing of criminals. "Algorithms are everywhere," says mathematician and data scientist Cathy O'Neil. "They sort and separate the winners from the losers. The winners get the job or a good credit card offer. The losers don't even get an interview or they pay more for insurance. We're being scored with secret formulas that we don't understand that often don't have systems of appeal."[27] For example, many companies and nonprofit organizations run credit reports on prospective employees. The companies reason that a person with a history of meeting financial obligations is more likely to be a better employee than a person who misses payments or is in deep debt.

> "We're being scored with secret formulas that we don't understand that often don't have systems of appeal."[27]
>
> —Cathy O'Neil, a mathematician and data scientist

The criminal justice system also uses algorithms to measure the likelihood an individual will relapse into criminal behavior. However, these decisions can turn into self-fulfilling prophecies. A person classified as high risk by the algorithm is often given a long sentence, and because of the long sentence, that person will find it harder to find a job when released from prison. Such a person, experts say, is more likely than those with shorter sentences to commit another crime. This makes it appear that the algorithm made an accurate prediction, but actually it played a role in determining the final outcome. "The algorithms are like shiny new toys that we can't resist using," says O'Neil. "We trust them so much that we project meaning on to them."[28]

Using computers to analyze, or mine, personal data is a major privacy concern, according to the President's Council of Advisors on Science and Technology (PCAST). "By data mining and other

Car dealerships and other businesses that offer loans obtain credit reports to evaluate a potential borrower's ability to pay off a loan. Some privacy experts object to the use of these reports to make decisions that affect a person's future.

kinds of analytics, non-obvious and sometimes private information can be derived from data that, at the time of its collection, seems to raise no, or manageable, privacy issues," states a report by PCAST. The report continues:

> The same data and analytics that provide benefits to individuals and society if used appropriately can also create potential harms—threats to individual privacy according to privacy norms both widely shared and personal. For example, large-scale analysis of research on disease, together with health data from electronic medical records and genomic information, might lead to better and timelier

treatment for individuals but also to inappropriate disqual-
ification for insurance or jobs. GPS tracking of individuals
might lead to better community-based public transporta-
tion facilities, but also to inappropriate use of the where-
abouts of individuals.[29]

Watched by the Internet of Things

The ability of companies to know a person's every move will only
increase in the future due to the staggering growth in electronic
sensors and devices connected to the Internet of Things (IoT).
The computer networking company Cisco estimates that the total
number of so-called smart devices connected to the Internet—
including televisions, refrigerators, washing machines, home light-
ing systems, climate control systems, medical and health care
equipment, and vehicles—will reach 35 billion in 2019. Cisco estimates that 1 trillion networked sensors will be online by 2022.

Most of these devices send information over the Internet to remote computers, which then make decisions about what to do
with the devices. For example, information from a sensor about the
temperature of a room can cause a remote computer to turn off the
heat or air-conditioning in a home to save energy. However, some of
the information sent by in-home devices is highly personal. For example, some sensors are used to monitor a person's health. These
devices send data about the user's heart rate, breathing, perspira-
tion, and other physical functions over the Internet to smartphone
apps and sometimes on to health care companies. In general, the
companies that create the sensors and apps control the information the devices generate. As a result, the private information can
be sent to people or organizations without the user knowing about
it, and those companies can use the information in ways that can
affect the person negatively. For example, privacy expert Brian Katz
has found that information from wearable devices that send data
about a person's physical fitness activity—known as Fitbits—can
end up in the hands of a person's employer. "A lot of companies

give out Fitbits, for example, to gather data about employees that's used for insurance purposes," says Katz. A computer analysis of a person's private fitness data could reveal a health condition that has no bearing on the employee's work performance but that the employer perceives as being a potential problem. "If your manager knows about it, do they act on it?"[30] Katz asks.

Some countries have attempted to regulate the use of private information by employers. In the European Union (EU), for example, companies must notify individuals of any data gathered about them. Processing the data with algorithms can only be done for legitimate purposes, such as investigating fraud or other criminal activity. The EU also has strict rules for sharing such data. The United States is more lenient, according to Joseph Jerome, a privacy expert at the Center for Democracy & Technology in Washington, DC. "Basically employers can get away with anything they want so long as they're providing some kind of notice of consent,"[31] says Jerome.

As the use of sensors and smart devices grows, big data applications will be able to put together even more information about people, their locations, and their activities—even in the home. For example, researchers at Princeton University have shown that a detailed profile of a person's daily activities can be gleaned just from the levels of traffic being generated by IoT devices in the home. These activities can include sleeping patterns, exercise routines, and movements within the home. The person or company doing the spying does not have to intercept the content being sent from the devices to understand what the person is doing. All that is needed is a record of when the devices are turning on and off and sending data. As a result, encrypting the data

> "The same data and analytics that provide benefits to individuals and society if used appropriately can also create potential harms—threats to individual privacy according to privacy norms both widely shared and personal."[29]
>
> —The President's Council of Advisors on Science and Technology

being sent by the devices offers no protection to the user. "An ISP [Internet service provider] or other network observer can infer privacy sensitive in-home activities by analyzing Internet traffic from smart homes containing commercially available IoT devices *even when the devices use encryption*," write the researchers.

> Traffic rates from a Sense sleep monitor revealed consumer sleep patterns, traffic rates from a Belkin WeMo switch [to control devices from a smartphone] revealed when a physical appliance in a smart home is turned on or off, and traffic rates from a Nest Cam Indoor security camera revealed when a user is actively monitoring the camera feed or when the camera detects motion in a user's home.[32]

Recording Conversations in the Home

In addition to simple data about a person's movements and activities in the home, devices in the IoT routinely record audio and send it over the Internet to remote servers located in large clusters known as the cloud. The most popular of these devices are smart speakers such as Amazon Echo and Google Home. Like smart televisions, game consoles, and toys, these devices are equipped with microphones designed to pick up the human voice at varying distances. However, unlike the other devices, which require the user to push a button to be heard by the device, smart speakers are always on, waiting to be activated by a trigger phrase or wake word. In the case of Amazon Echo, the wake word is *Alexa*, the name of the company's intelligent personal assistant (IPA); in the case of Google Home, the trigger phrase is *Okay Google*.

When users ask questions of the IPA, the question is recorded by the smart speaker and sent over the Internet to a remote computer for processing. For example, the user might ask the IPA a question such as "What will the weather be like tomorrow?" or, as demonstrated in an Amazon Echo television commercial, "How do you spell *tyrannosaurus*?" The processing center forwards the question to a weather bureau or search engine and then sends the answer to the user, using the speaker's voice simulator. IPAs connected to smart devices in the home can turn lights on and off, lock doors, and even warm up the family car.

The entire IPA setup concerns privacy experts. "The new-found privacy conundrum presented by installing a device that can literally listen to everything you're saying represents a chilling new development in the age of internet-connected things," writes Adam Clark Estes, a writer for the website Gizmodo. "By buying a smart speaker, you're effectively paying money to let a huge tech company surveil you."[33] The concerns are threefold, says Jay Stanley, a senior policy analyst for the ACLU. "Overall, digital assistants and other IoT devices create a triple threat to privacy: from government, corporations, and hackers."[34]

Personal smart speakers, such as Amazon Echo (pictured), are always on, listening and recording. Privacy experts worry that private information could be abused by businesses, governments, and hackers.

Like telephone records, the recordings made by smart speakers are saved by a private company. As such, they could fall under the third-party doctrine if law enforcement officials wanted to hear them. This concerns the ACLU. "We fear that some government agencies will try to argue that they do not need a warrant to access this kind of data," writes Stanley. "We believe the Constitution is clear, and that, at a minimum, law enforcement needs a warrant based on probable cause to access conversations recorded in the home using such devices. But more protections are needed."[35]

Some cell phones also feature an always on mode for interacting with IPAs such as Apple's Siri. US Supreme Court justice Sonia Sotomayor raised concerns about both location finding and eavesdropping through the IoT in the oral arguments of *Carpenter*:

> As I understand it, a cell phone can be pinged in your bedroom. It can be pinged at your doctor's office. It can ping you in the most intimate details of your life. Presumably at some point even in a dressing room as you're undressing. So I am not beyond the belief that someday a provider could turn on my cell phone and listen to my conversations.[36]

The Nothing-to-Hide Argument

Some people are not concerned about what their business records may contain because they believe they have not done anything wrong and have nothing to hide from companies, employers, or government authorities. Former Google chief executive officer (CEO) Eric Schmidt echoed this idea in 2005: "If you have something that you don't want anyone to know, maybe you shouldn't be doing it in the first place, but if you really need that kind of privacy, the reality is that search engines including Google do retain this information for some time."[37] Privacy advocate and whistle-blower Edward Snowden blasted this kind of thinking in an address to an Australian audience in 2016. Reminding the audience of the Nazi regime that terrorized civilians and suppressed its opponents during the 1930s and 1940s, Snowden said that if someone "is saying 'if you have nothing to hide, then you have nothing to fear' you need to stand up and remind them that that is literally a piece of Nazi propaganda advanced by the minister of propaganda, Joseph Goebbels." Snowden continued,

> "We don't want a police state, we don't want a security state, we don't want to be watched for no reason."[38]
>
> —Privacy advocate Edward Snowden

That's not something that we should have people in open, liberal democracies advancing as our policy choice. We don't want a police state, we don't want a security state, we don't want to be watched for no reason and it's not because we have nothing to hide. . . . If we don't [oppose it], we have lost something fundamental, we have lost not just a single right, we have lost all of them. We have lost liberty.[38]

CHAPTER 3

Criminal Hacking

The same digital information that sometimes has value for law enforcement and businesses can be even more valuable to criminals who can personally profit from it. Computer experts known as hackers specialize in overcoming security measures to access computer files and gain control of devices for a range of illegal uses, including identity theft, blackmail, and document forging.

Exposing Private Records

A person is much more likely to have his or her privacy invaded by a criminal than by anyone else. According to a report by Risk Based Security, businesses reported more than five thousand data breaches in 2017, putting an astounding 7.8 billion customer records into criminal hands. These records include not only names and addresses but also social security numbers, credit card numbers, passwords, and more. For example, Equifax, one of the three major credit bureaus in the United States, announced in July 2017 that hackers had accessed the social security numbers, birth dates, and driver's license numbers of up to 143 million US consumers. In March 2018 Equifax announced that an additional 2.4 million consumers were affected by the breach, bringing the total number of people whose data was compromised to more than 147 million. According to Risk Based Security, the latest hacks brought the total number of known security breaches to more than 28,800. These breaches exposed more than 19 billion computer records to hackers, invading the privacy of billions of people worldwide.

As large as the numbers of reported breaches are, they do not include all of the successful cyberattacks that have occurred. Many security breaches go undetected for months or even years, and many are never reported. "We are extremely confident that breaches are undiscovered and under-reported, and we don't know the full scope," says Eva Casey Velasquez, the CEO of the Identity Theft Resource Center. Referring to the enormous number of reported breaches, she adds, "This isn't the worst-case scenario we are looking at; this is the best-case scenario."[39]

In January 2018 Senators Elizabeth Warren and Mark Warner introduced legislation to hold credit reporting agencies accountable for data breaches that expose information that they were entrusted with keeping private. If passed, the Data Breach Prevention and Compensation Act of 2018 will establish an office of cybersecurity within the Federal Trade Commission (FTC) to supervise data protection in the credit reporting industry and impose mandatory fines for breaches of consumer data. "Under this legislation, Equifax would have had to pay at least a $1.5 billion penalty for their failure to protect Americans' personal information," Senator Warren said in a statement. "To ensure robust recovery for affected consumers, the bill would also require the FTC to use 50 percent of its penalty to compensate consumers and would increase penalties in cases of woefully inadequate cybersecurity or if a CRA [credit reporting agency] fails to timely notify the FTC of a breach."[40]

Businesses are not the only targets for hackers. Cybercriminals attack individuals as well, often using malicious computer programs known as malware. The most common form of malware attack is known as ransomware. According to the research firm Malwarebytes, ransomware accounted for 60 percent of all malware infections. The number of ransomware attacks surged in 2017, increasing by more than 62 percent over 2016. "Ransomware is emerging as the latest tool of choice for cybercriminals,"[41] states a Malwarebytes report.

In a ransomware attack, the invading software program encrypts the user's private computer files, making them impossible

In January 2018 Senator Elizabeth Warren introduced legislation to hold credit reporting agencies accountable for data breaches. The new legislation calls for a new office of cybersecurity within the Federal Trade Commission.

to read and use. The malware then launches a message on the screen that informs the victim that the only way to decrypt the files is to pay a ransom for decrypting software, known as a decryption key. Turning off the computer or attempting to rid the device of the malware will lead to the destruction of the decryption key, the message warns. Needing access to their files, most victims click on a link provided by the malware and authorize payment to the hacker's bank account. "Over the last few years attackers realized that instead of going through these elaborate hacks—phishing for passwords, breaking into accounts, stealing information, and then selling the data on the internet's black market for pennies per record—they could simply target individuals and businesses and treat them like an ATM,"[42] says Brian Beyer, the CEO of security firm Red Canary.

Phishing for Personal Information

Hackers often gain access to a person's private information by sending fraudulent e-mails, a technique known as phishing. In a phishing attack, the victim receives an official-looking e-mail, often from a recognizable source, such as the Internal Revenue Service, Netflix, eBay, Google, or Microsoft. Many phishing e-mails contain a warning that one of the user's accounts has been hacked and the user must change his or her password immediately. The e-mail provides a link to a fake website that asks for the person to log in using the correct password. When the victim does so, the hacker uses the password to unlock the real account. Once inside, the hacker changes the password immediately so the real user cannot access it. The hacker can then copy the e-mails or look through them for sensitive information, such as other passwords, account numbers, and banking information.

This is exactly the kind of attack that led John Podesta, the head of Hillary Clinton's 2016 presidential campaign, to surrender access to his Gmail account to hackers. According to the *Atlantic* magazine, Podesta received an e-mail disguised as an alert from Google advising him to change his password. An information technology staffer advised Podesta that the e-mail was legitimate. The campaign manager clicked on the fake link and entered his Gmail password. The hackers downloaded thousands of confidential e-mails, which were eventually leaked to the press. Many political experts believe that the release of Podesta's e-mails hurt the credibility of Clinton and contributed to her narrow defeat in the 2016 presidential election.

One of the problems with stopping phishing attacks is that the fake websites are not online very long, which makes it hard to catch the criminals behind them. "The longest-running phishing site was active less than two days, and the shortest was only 15 minutes," states cybersecurity firm Webroot in its 2017 annual security report. "Eighty-four percent of all phishing sites were active for less than 24 hours."[43]

An Expanding Attack Surface

One reason for the surge in successful cyberattacks is that the number of vulnerable devices is growing at a phenomenal rate, mainly due to the rapid expansion of the IoT. "The proliferation of mobile devices creates more endpoints to protect," explains the *Cisco 2017 Annual Cybersecurity Report*. "As businesses embrace digitization—and the Internet of Everything (IoE) begins to take shape—defenders will have even more to worry about. The attack surface will only expand, giving adversaries more space to operate."[44]

Any device connected to a network, no matter how small its computer, can provide a way for a hacker to enter a system. In fact, the smaller the computer, the less secure it usually is because it does not have the processing power to run sophisticated security software. This is exactly what happened in a series of security breaches in which hackers breached the security of ten hospitals in 2016. The hackers penetrated the hospitals' computer networks through computerized diagnostic equipment, including X-ray machines, magnetic resonance imaging machines, and blood gas analyzers. Such devices are equipped with small computers that process the diagnostic data and relay it to larger computers used by laboratory technicians and doctors. However, the computers in the equipment are too small—and in many cases too old—to run effective security software. "The standard cyber security environment set up in the hospital, regardless of how effective it might be, cannot access the internal software operations of medical devices," explains Carl Wright, the executive vice president and general manager at TrapX Security, the firm that investigated the hospital security breaches. Once the hackers obtained the proper log-in credentials, they were able to sneak into the network and copy sensitive hospital

> "As businesses embrace digitization—and the Internet of Everything (IoE) begins to take shape—defenders will have even more to worry about."[44]
>
> —Cisco 2017 Annual Cybersecurity Report

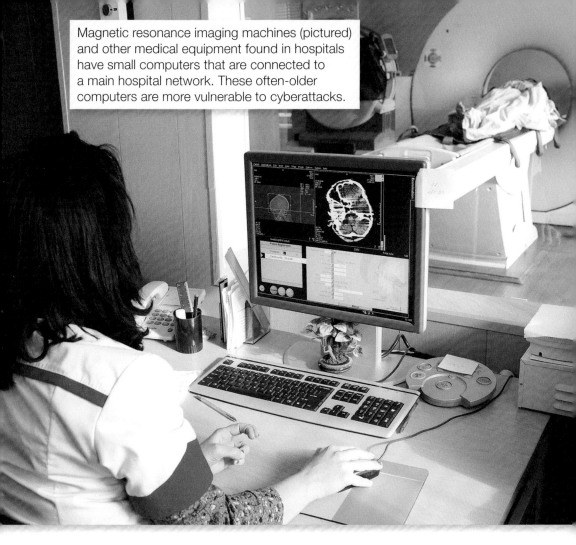

Magnetic resonance imaging machines (pictured) and other medical equipment found in hospitals have small computers that are connected to a main hospital network. These often-older computers are more vulnerable to cyberattacks.

records. "The records enable fraudulent access to the victim's financial accounts including bank accounts, credit card accounts and more," explained Moshe Ben-Simon, the cofounder and vice president of TrapX Security. "Medical records are the top targets for cyber attackers."[45]

Turning the IoT Against Its Users

The IoT is spreading beyond businesses to private homes, and hackers are not far behind. The vulnerability of home computer networks was illustrated by eleven-year-old computer whiz Reuben Paul, who wowed an audience of security experts at a 2017 HaxPo security conference in the Netherlands by first hacking

Hacktivism Benefits Civil Liberties

Most people think of hackers as destructive cybercriminals, but technology journalist Adam Shepherd argues that some hackers use their skills to demonstrate that private information is not being properly defended and to fight for online civil liberties.

> The term "hacktivism" has become increasingly prominent in recent years, commonly accompanied by images of hoodie-clad figures sporting the now-iconic Guy Fawkes mask. But what exactly is hacktivism?
>
> Hacktivism refers to the use of computer hacking to achieve political and sociological goals. It takes many forms and is used by individuals and groups of many different beliefs and ideologies. Hacktivists often share common tactics. One popular strategy, due to the low level of technical skill needed to pull it off, is to take down offending websites with DDOS attacks. Hackers also frequently steal sensitive data and dump it onto the internet, either to punish an organisation for something or to publicly release information that a hacker thinks should not be kept secret. . . .
>
> Modern hacktivism, however, has been defined mainly by the group known as 'Anonymous.'. . . Anonymous has also been heavily involved in various campaigns to foil attacks on internet freedoms. The group mounted significant efforts to fight the Stop Online Piracy Act (SOPA) and the Protect Intellectual Property Act (PIPA), both of which were accused of being efforts to censor the web.

Adam Shepherd, "What Is Hacktivism?," IT Pro, January 2, 2018. www.itpro.co.uk.

their phones and then using one of the phones to access a small computer inside his robotic teddy bear. "From airplanes to automobiles, from smart phones to smart homes, anything or any toy can be part of the Internet of Things (IOT)," Paul told the audience. "From terminators to teddy bears, anything or any toy can be weaponized."[46]

Hacktivism Threatens Privacy

Tom Sorell is a professor of politics and philosophy at the University of Warwick in England. He believes that hacktivists violate the privacy of individuals and expose them to danger.

> Not all Wikileaks information is leaked. Instead of being provided by insiders, some of it is stolen by outsiders and then given to Wikileaks. For example, internal emails from an American security intelligence company, Stratfor, that were relatively recently disclosed, came to Wikileaks not from company employees but from the cyberactivist group Anonymous. How Anonymous came to choose this company as a target is unclear, and, as in the case of some of the material included in the diplomatic cables, it is quite a varied set of emails, some of no obvious public interest at all. More significantly, however, some of those published contained identifying information and therefore exposed employees and others to cyber-hostility or worse from those who are likely to vilify organizations targeted by Wikileaks and Anonymous. Equally significantly, Wikileaks published this material despite its stated commitment to UDHR [the Universal Declaration of Human Rights], and despite the UDHR containing a right to privacy (article 12) that clearly encompasses personal emails, especially when their publication harms the reputations of innocent people.

Tom Sorell, "Human Rights and Hacktivism: The Cases of Wikileaks and Anonymous," *Journal of Human Rights Practice*, vol. 7, no. 3, November 2015. https://doi.org.

The Austin, Texas, sixth-grader demonstrated what he meant by using his Raspberry Pi computer to scan the room for mobile phones with their Bluetooth wireless networking devices turned on. Bluetooth is used for connecting many IoT devices, but it is also known to have security flaws. Paul found dozens of Bluetooth-enabled mobile phones, overcame their security, and displayed the phone numbers on a large screen suspended above the stage. Paul then used one of the phones to hack into the teddy bear, which also had a Bluetooth connection. "Most internet-connected things have a blue-tooth functionality," Paul said after the demonstration. "I basically showed how I could connect to it, and send commands to it."[47] Paul later tweeted about his experience. "It was fun but I hope people did not miss the message," he wrote. "Secure IoT before the Internet of Toys becomes the Internet of Threats."[48]

> "Secure IoT before the Internet of Toys becomes the Internet of Threats."[48]
>
> —Reuben Paul, student and cybersecurity expert

The vulnerability of the IoT was further demonstrated by the 2017 hack of 820,000 accounts of people who had purchased the talking plush toys called CloudPets. The toys are equipped with small digital devices that enabled them to receive messages from smartphones and say the words that were sent, usually by parents, grandparents, and others close to the children who own the toys. Because the toys' computers were small and seemingly inconsequential, the owners were not especially concerned about security. Many chose passwords that were easy to remember rather than ones that would be difficult for a hacker to overcome. "Because there were no rules, lots of people created bad passwords," says Troy Hunt, a cybersecurity expert who studied the CloudPets case. "I did an exercise and found it was really easy to create them. Lots of people were using the password Cloudpets because that's what people do."[49] Hunt found some passwords consisted of only one letter. Once hackers gained access to the toys, they could connect to other devices on the home network, including smartphones, tablets, and computers, obtaining bank and credit card account numbers, passwords, and other sensitive information.

Turning Cameras on the Owners

Some hackers profit from invading home networks not by stealing account information but by spying on the victims and posting images of their activities on the Internet. Typically, the hackers gain control of a surveillance camera or child monitor, known as a nanny cam, and take videos inside a home without permission. In 2016 Katerina Manoff, a blogger in Houston, Texas, who writes about family issues, received a tip about a smartphone app that featured live feeds from various nearby homes. Alarmed by the potential invasions of privacy, she checked to see whether the story was true. "Just a regular mom, I was able to take three minutes, and I was looking into some little girl's room," Manoff told CBS News. "I mean, I felt like a creep doing it."[50]

Manoff posted a picture from the live feed on social media, hoping to find the family and let them know their privacy was being invaded. Dozens of others on social media reposted the image, and within twenty-four hours the effort to find the homeowner succeeded. "I have cameras to protect my kids and I kind of feel like I failed them," said the mother whose nanny cam had been hacked. "We didn't protect them. We actually put them in harm's way."[51]

Using in-home cameras to spy on people is big business, according to security expert Bryan Lagard. "People just don't realize that there are websites dedicated to finding open webcams and posting the footage," says Lagard. A couple in Rochester, Minnesota, learned this for themselves when they discovered images from their toddler's bedroom displayed on a website based in the Netherlands in 2015. Pictures from their home were displayed along with thousands of others. "You can literally just sort by whatever country suits your fancy and sort by whatever rooms that you fancy," said the Rochester woman, describing the Dutch website. "It's not just nurseries. It's people's living rooms, their bedrooms, their kitchens. Every place that people think is sacred and private in their home is being accessed. . . . It's pretty sick."[52]

> "I have [surveillance] cameras to protect my kids and I kind of feel like I failed them. We didn't protect them. We actually put them in harm's way."[51]
>
> —A Houston mother whose nanny cam feed was hacked and posted online

Security Standards for the IoT

Part of the problem with the IoT is that most consumers do not perceive threats from things like their refrigerators or surveillance cameras. As a result, they do not read the security instructions fully or take time to create strong passwords. "The approach of letting consumers worry about the security of their own devices has clearly failed," writes Chris Duckett, an editor with the technology news website ZDNet. "There is a percentage that are capable of knowing what is on their [home computing] network and are able to prevent [their devices] from going rogue, but the vast majority of consumers do not have the faintest idea of how to control their network."[53]

The other problem is that many makers of smart devices are more concerned with cashing in on consumer demand than they are with what happens to the devices after they are sold. For

Pictured on the left is a camera-equipped baby monitor. Some hackers will invade home networks to gain access to these and other types of cameras to spy on unsuspecting victims and sometimes even post the images online.

example, researchers at the security firm Bitdefender tested a popular security camera in 2017 and found that it contained a design flaw. The researchers staged an attack on the device to prove they could gain control of it via the Internet. "This . . . attack confirms once again that most Internet of Things devices are trivial to exploit because of improper quality assurance," stated the Bitdefender researchers. Made by Chinese manufacturer Shenzhen Neo Electronics, the cameras sell for as little as thirty-nine dollars each and have gained a widespread following, with at least 175,000 installations worldwide. Because of the design flaw, hackers do not have to know or even guess the camera's password. "By manipulating the login and password fields of the form, the attacker can inject commands and trick the camera into executing code as it attempts to perform the authentication,"[54] said Bogdan Botezatu, a senior analyst at Bitdefender. Once inside the camera, the hacker can use it to watch the home or gain access to other devices on the same network.

John Stewart, the chief security officer for Cisco, believes that new products connecting to the IoT should meet basic security standards, just as electrical appliances are required to meet electrical safety standards. He worries that without at least minimal security measures in the IoT, hackers could use them to overload networks and cause them to crash, an attack known as a distributed denial of service (DDoS). "If nothing else," Stewart says, "you could have something like diagnostic instrumentation on your refrigerator to determine, 'Is it chilling the eggs?' but 'Is it also generating spam or launching a DDoS attack?'"[55]

Attacking the Intelligent Personal Assistants

Privacy experts worry that hackers will soon be able to find out even more about a person by accessing an important device linked to the IoT: the IPA. These voice-activated devices can interpret speech and carry out user commands related to the Internet and the IoT. The best-known IPAs are Amazon's Alexa,

Google's Google Assistant, Apple's Siri, Microsoft's Cortana, and Viv Labs' Viv. IPAs linked to smart devices on a home network can turn on lights, play music from a smartphone or tablet, or run hot water for a bath. Alexa can be used to order and pay for products from Amazon simply by voice command. IPAs can also search the Internet and connect to various data centers, such as weather bureaus, to provide answers to virtually any question. But behind the convenience lurk several privacy concerns.

One the biggest potential problems with IPAs is that they record the commands they receive and send them to remote computers for processing. The process is instantaneous, but Amazon keeps the recordings to improve the accuracy of its speech-recognition systems and to better understand how Alexa is used. A hacker who intercepts these messages or gains access to Amazon's library of recordings would know some of the most intimate details of the user's daily life. "Users will impress their friends by using speech commands to switch on the TV, preheat the oven, or pop open the trunk of the car," writes Hiawatha Bray, a technology reporter for the *Boston Globe*. "And each of these actions is now recorded in a data center perhaps halfway around the world. Inside your nondigital home, privacy is the default setting. In the IoT world, it's the other way around."[56] Apple's Siri also stores recordings, but they are indexed by randomly generated code, not the users' names. Apple says it destroys the recordings after two years.

The app that controls Alexa keeps a log of the user's activities, but it lets the user decide what to save and what to delete. The Aspen Institute, a think tank in Washington, DC, thinks IPA makers should go further. It suggests that the device makers should allow users to not share their usage information with manufactur-

> "Inside your nondigital home, privacy is the default setting. In the IoT world, it's the other way around."[56]
>
> —Hiawatha Bray, a technology reporter for the *Boston Globe*

ers or third parties such as advertisers. Bray agrees. "I should be able to remotely control my air conditioner without telling Whirlpool or Kenmore about it,"[57] he writes.

Mobilizing an Army of Devices

Cybersecurity experts also worry that hackers will be able to mobilize peoples' home devices to mount a large-scale DDoS attack on Internet service providers, causing portions of the Internet and all of the connected devices to fail. This type of attack would invade everyone's privacy because it could destroy valuable computer records, cause food to spoil by turning off refrigerators, and even affect health by turning off heating and air-conditioning systems and disrupting medical devices. "We can talk about refrigerators sending spam all day long, but the truth of it is, what we really want to be focusing on is exactly how many control systems are ensuring that the pharmaceutical industry is producing the right pill for you, the power is going to your house correctly, the water is not contaminated and is flowing at the right pressure,"[58] says Cisco's John Stewart.

The hackers might demand some sort of ransom to stop the DDoS attack, but more likely such an attack would be carried out by one nation to cripple another. Network security software maker Arbor Networks detected 6.1 million DDoS attacks in the first 272 days of 2017. That figure breaks down to 22,426 attacks per day, 934 per hour, and 15 per minute. Most of these attacks are aimed at businesses, but governments have been targeted as well. For example, on August 9, 2016, a DDoS attack overwhelmed the Australian census bureau website in the middle of its online national census. The breakdown was so bad that the government pulled the website offline and postponed the census.

One of the most serious targets of a DDoS attack is an electrical grid because it could knock out not only lights and air-conditioning but also essential equipment of all kinds. Hackers have already launched DDoS attacks on electrical grids around the world. In 2014 suspected Russian hackers launched a DDoS attack against the electrical grid of Ukraine, causing crippling blackouts that lasted several hours. In 2015 Russian-based hackers hit the power grids of the Baltic states of Lithuania, Latvia, and Estonia, not causing blackouts but disrupting operations. In May 2017 the international news agency Reuters reported that hackers launched more exploratory attacks against the Baltic states. "On a daily basis there are DDoS attacks designed to probe network architecture, so it could well be possible that something (serious) could take place later on,"[59] a North Atlantic Treaty Organization (NATO) official told Reuters.

Were a hack of the electrical grid successful, it would reach into the businesses and homes of thousands or even millions of people, violating their right to be left alone. Electronic devices and records could be destroyed, security systems that protect people's privacy could be rendered useless, and medical equipment that monitors and even maintains health could be shut down. "We've got to pay attention and wake up," says Stewart, adding:

> If we continue down the path at the pace that we're going, then we're going to have one of those years where we're not going to be able to say, 'Yep, we made it through another year, and it was tough, but we did a couple of things and we're OK.' We're going to hurt someday, and that's what scares me—that if we don't change the way we've chosen to go after these problems, then somebody's going to get hurt.[60]

CHAPTER 4

Social Media Profiling

Every day hundreds of millions of Internet users around the world voluntarily share pictures, videos, messages, and personal information such as birthdays and anniversaries on social networks such as Facebook and Instagram. The terms of service for these social networking companies allow them to use information collected from users in a number of ways. Privacy experts believe that some of the ways in which the social networks use this information pose a threat to privacy—and thus to the civil liberties of their users.

Monitoring What People Post

One way that social networking websites invade the privacy of users is by using automated programs to monitor what people post. For example, in June 2017 Instagram announced that it would use big data analytics to search for rude and intimidating comments in order to prevent cyberbullying. The announcement followed the release of a survey by the antibullying charity Ditch the Label. The survey found that 42 percent of twelve- to twenty-five-year-olds in the United Kingdom reported having been bullied on Instagram. The big data algorithm known as DeepText uses machine learning to find the offensive comments and delete them before anyone has seen them. "Machine learning algorithms have proven to be effective ways to detect hate speech and cyberbullying,"[61] says social media reporter Tom Davidson.

Some people say that DeepText is used not only to eliminate nasty comments but also to silence opinions. In 2016 the politically conservative comedy group known as Toughen Up America complained that its Instagram profile was suspended ahead of the 2016 US elections without reason, notice, or the possibility of appeal. Instagram's chief executive officer, Kevin Systrom, denies that DeepText is used to silence opinions. "We're not here to curb free speech. We're not here to curb fun conversations between friends. But we are here to make sure we're attacking the problem of bad comments on Instagram,"[62] Systrom told *Wired* magazine.

> "We're not here to curb free speech. We're not here to curb fun conversations between friends. But we are here to make sure we're attacking the problem of bad comments on Instagram."[62]
>
> —Kevin Systrom, the CEO of Instagram

Instagram also uses automated programs, called bots, to enforce its community guidelines for hashtags. For example, the company was criticized in 2015 for banning the hashtag *#curvy*, which Instagram explained was being used to search for material that violated the company's policies against sexually suggestive photos. "This adds to Instagram's long history of banning users and terms for, what many view as, arbitrary reasons,"[63] observed *Time* magazine. In the face of mounting criticism, Instagram dropped the #curvy ban after about two weeks. However, the company continues to ban hashtags about eating disorders, self-harm, and the sale of firearms.

Social Media as a Public Forum

The monitoring of social media posts and the removal of content raises civil liberties issues both in the area of privacy and free speech. In the 2017 case *Packingham v. North Carolina*, the Supreme Court ruled that social networking websites like Instagram and Facebook are public forums in which speech is protected from government interference. "While in the past there may have been difficulty in identifying the most important places (in a spatial sense) for the exchange of views, today the answer is clear. It is cyberspace—the 'vast democratic forums of the Internet' in general, and social media in particular," wrote Justice Anthony Kennedy for the majority. The case arose from a North Carolina law that banned registered sex offenders from joining the most popular social networking websites. "To foreclose access to social media altogether is to prevent the user from engaging in the legitimate exercise of First Amendment rights,"[64] stated the court.

To prevent cyberbullying, the social media site Instagram uses big data analytics to search for rude and intimidating comments. Some believe this represents an invasion of privacy.

Generally speaking, the First Amendment applies to governmental restrictions on free speech, not to limits placed by private companies. On their own premises, businesses are free to limit the speech of their employees and customers. However, in a 1995 case the high court ruled that private electronic networks, such as cable television channels, can be designated a public forum and thus be governed by the First Amendment. Even when a private company, such as a cable company, is limiting access to material, this can be a violation of civil liberties. The court's ruling in *Packingham* suggests that social media falls in the same category.

Instagram not only bans certain hashtags, but it also deletes photos that violate the company's guidelines. For example, it has deleted topless photos by model Naomi Campbell, pop singer Miley Cyrus, and comedian Chelsea Handler. Not all photos removed by the bots involve nudity, however. In 2015 poet Rupi Kaur posted a photo of a fully clothed woman whose clothing and bedsheets were stained with what appeared to be menstrual blood. After the photo was taken down the first time, Kaur reposted it, and it was removed a second time. "Thank you Instagram for providing me with the exact response my work was created to critique," wrote Kaur, commenting on the incident. "I will not apologize for not feeding the ego and pride of misogynist society."[65] When social media websites delete user content, they are taking actions that would not be allowed under the First Amendment if the government were doing the same thing. Although private companies are not yet legally barred from taking such actions, Kaur and others believe they are violating the rights of the users.

Sneaky Ways of Building the Network

Sometimes social networking companies invade user privacy as the companies try to increase the number of participants. For example, when people join a social network, they usually are given the option to import contact lists from their cell phones, e-mail, or another social network. This allows the new user to quickly find matches with friends already in the network. Many users take this step to save time, not realizing that they are sharing a friend's contact information with the social network without that person's consent. Some social networking users have found their phone numbers filled in on their profiles, even though they never provided

Many social media sites delete photos or images that violate their policies. Instagram deleted a topless photo of pop singer Miley Cyrus (pictured in 2017) that was posted to its site.

the network with their numbers. The social networking company has filled in the data from the contact lists of the user's friends.

In 2016 Facebook came under fire for testing new ways of building its following without the consent of its users. Technology journalist Kashmir Hill reported that the networking giant was using a process similar to the one at issue in *Carpenter v. United States* to increase participation in the network—using cell phone location to reach out to more people. "A Facebook spokesperson told me that users' smartphone location data was among the signals that the social network uses to suggest 'People You May Know' in real life,"[66] wrote Hill. Facebook admitted to the practice, but the company added that it had combined location data with other factors, such as employment backgrounds and education information. The company said it was not a standard practice but

Facebook Violated the Privacy of Its Users

In May 2017 the Commission Nationale de l'Informatique et des Libertés (CNIL), the French government's data protection watchdog agency, found that Facebook violated the privacy of Facebook users when it used their private data for ad targeting:

> The . . . Committee finds that the Facebook group does not have a legal basis to [use] the information it has on account holders to display targeted advertising. It also finds that the Facebook group engages in unlawful tracking, via the [cookies], of internet users. The cookie banner and the mention of information collected "on and outside Facebook" do not allow users to clearly understand that their personal data are systematically collected as soon as they navigate on a third-party website that includes a social plug in.

Autoriteit Persoonsgegevens et al., "Common Statement by the Contact Group of the Data Protection Authorities of the Netherlands, France, Spain, Hamburg, and Belgium," May 16, 2017. https://autoriteit persoonsgegevens.nl.

Facebook Did Not Violate the Privacy of Its Users

Facebook, the world's largest social network, disputed the finding of the French data protection agency (CNIL) that it violated the privacy of its users when it used their profile data for ad targeting. In a statement e-mailed to Reuters news service, Facebook responded: "We take note of the CNIL's decision with which we respectfully disagree. At Facebook, putting people in control of their privacy is at the heart of everything we do. Over recent years, we've simplified our policies further to help people understand how we use information to make Facebook better."

Quoted in Reuters Staff, "Facebook Fined 150,000 Euros by French Data Watchdog," May 16, 2017. www.reuters.com.

only a four-week test. Still, the experiment struck some observers as an invasion of privacy. "Did it ask permission from users involved in the trial to do that? Did it publicly admit to doing so?" asked Thomas Fox-Brewster, a writer for *Forbes* who covers digital privacy and security. "The answers appear to be no and no."[67]

Profiling for Advertisers

Social networks try to increase their size and build up connections among users not just to make the world a friendlier, more connected place but also to make money. Early social networking websites charged fees for using them, and some, like LinkedIn and Classmates, still charge for full access to the content. Most social networks make money by charging advertisers fees to place ads on the websites. The more followers the network has, and the more time users spend on the website, the more advertising the company can attract.

"Did [Facebook] ask permission from users involved in the trial to do that? Did it publicly admit to doing so? The answers appear to be no and no."[67]

—Thomas Fox-Brewster, a writer for *Forbes*

Advertisers normally are seeking to reach people with specific wants and needs that might lead them to buy the advertiser's product or service. Knowing that, social networking companies gather all kinds of details from users and employ the information to target the ads. For example, Facebook users often list their birth dates, locations, relationships, occupations, former employers, and schooling. A user might also detail various life events, such as a graduation, an engagement, a marriage, or the birth of a child. In addition to basic profile information, the user might indicate favorite sports teams, music, movies, television shows, books, apps, and games. Any Facebook pages that a person has liked, such as those for restaurants, clubs, resorts, stores, and groups also contribute to that person's profile. If, for example, an advertiser is trying to reach people under thirty who live in the Pacific Northwest and enjoy skiing, the social network will allow the advertiser to post ads on the pages of only the users who fit those three criteria. The social network does not provide the names of the people; it only allows for the placement of ads on pages or in news feeds of people who fit the desired profile.

Precise targeting allows the advertiser to achieve two things: first, to reach a desired audience, and second, to avoid spending money advertising to people who are unlikely to be interested in the advertiser's product or service. This is vastly different from traditional advertising, such as television and radio ads, which can only target ads on the basis of what program a person is watching or listening to. Precise targeting is particularly helpful to small businesses that may only want to advertise to people in a small geographic area. For example, a shop that carries toys and clothing for babies and toddlers can choose to spend its budget on social networking ads targeted only to people living within a few miles of the store and who have listed the birth of a child during the past six months, year, or two years.

Most people do not object to ads targeted to them in this way, but many are disturbed by seeing content so narrowly focused on their interests. A new parent might find a sudden rush of ads for baby formula or diapers a little disturbing because it raises questions about how many strangers know about the birth of his or her child. A sixty-year-old man who lists golf as a hobby might resent seeing ads promising to teach golf secrets for older golfers. A 2016 survey by the marketing research firm Drumbeat Marketing found that 72.73 percent of those surveyed found Facebook ads to be intrusive.

Retargeting

Being targeted on the basis of what a person reveals in a profile is one thing, but being targeted because of certain Internet searches or website visits can feel more invasive. This advertising technique is known as retargeting. *Forbes* contributor Theo Miller describes how it works:

> Let's say you spend all morning searching for the most artisanal kombucha [fermented tea] money can buy. You almost enter your credit card, but nothing's ever local enough for you.
>
> A day later, you read your horoscope on your favorite blog. There's a surprise waiting for you in the sidebar—a banner ad for that kombucha you decided not to buy. At first, it feels like fate. Your mind tricks you into believing your destiny is to buy that trendy elixir. Of course, it's not predestined, it's retargeting at work.[68]

Retargeting uses snippets of computer code, known as cookies, which are sent from websites to a person's computer, mobile phone, or tablet and are stored by the user's web browser. Some cookies make it possible for a website to recognize a returning visitor so that person does not have to log in every time he or she visits. Other cookies help a website track which pages a person visits and how long the user spends on each one. Advertising cookies sent when a person visits one website can be recognized when a person visits another. Since the cookie resides in the user's computer, it can trigger the placement of an ad related to the previous page as soon as the user visits a new website. For example, a person might look for a certain book on Amazon's website and then check his or her news feed on Facebook and immediately see an ad for that title. The immediacy of such ad placements can be unsettling because it seems as if the user is being watched as he or she travels from one website to another.

Psychometric Targeting

Some ads are on topics that are so personal that the person receiving them feels his or her privacy has been violated. This is especially true for mental health ads. For example, a Facebook user in California posted a picture and a birthday remembrance of his son, who had died three years earlier. Shortly afterward, the man began to see ads in his news feed from an organization that offers online counseling and therapy services. The ads contained headlines such as "Will I Ever Be Happy Again?," "Need Therapy?," and "Escape Your Mental Prison." "I didn't mind the first ad," says the man. "It was tastefully done, and I thought its appearance was nothing more than an odd coincidence. But as similar ads appeared over the following days, I realized I was being targeted for my grief. I felt my privacy was being invaded."[69]

The technique used to direct the counseling ads to the California father is known as psychometric targeting. This technique assigns numbers, or metrics, based on words appearing in a user's profile, events, comments, and posts. "Facebook has and does offer 'psychometric'-type targeting, where the goal is to define a subset of the marketing audience that an advertiser thinks is particularly susceptible to their message," writes Antonio Garcia-Martinez, a former Facebook product manager. "The question is not whether this can be done. It is whether Facebook should apply a moral filter to these decisions."[70]

Crossing an Ethical Boundary

While psychometric targeting may be acceptable for adults who consent to Facebook's terms of service, the company has come under fire for using the technique to target teens. In May 2017 the *Australian* newspaper reported on a confidential Facebook document that offered advertisers the opportunity to target 6.4 million teen users at "moments when young people need a confidence boost." The document suggested that Facebook could pinpoint users who had expressed feeling "worthless," "insecure," "defeated," and like a "failure."[71]

Many people were outraged that Facebook was prying into the lives of younger users and attempting to capitalize on the private feelings they expressed to their friends. "It's one thing to show makeup ads to people who follow Kylie Jenner on Instagram; it's another to use computational advertising techniques to sell flat-tummy tea to 14 year olds at the exact moment they're feeling their worst,"[72] observes Nitasha Tiku, a senior writer for *Wired* magazine. The idea that Facebook acted without specific consent from the teens being targeted for ads struck some users as a violation of their privacy. "This oversteps a boundary," says Jess, a nineteen-year-old Facebook user. "Facebook should be a safe space and it seems they are trying to invade that."[73]

> "Facebook should be a safe space and it seems they are trying to invade that."[73]
>
> —Jess, a nineteen-year-old Facebook user

Facebook issued a public statement confirming the existence of the advertising report, but the company denied the central charge. "Facebook does not offer tools to target people based on their emotional state," the statement read. Facebook added that the research, which included teens as young as fourteen, "was never used to target ads." The company stated that the analysis of the teens' posts and comments was not in line with its research policies. As a result, the company said, it would be "reviewing the details to correct the oversight."[74] Critics of Facebook were skeptical of the company's statement. "When Facebook said this was [an] aberration, we knew that was not true, because it squarely fits into what Facebook does all the time in terms of analyzing the emotional reactions of individuals,"[75]Jeff Chester, the executive director of the Center for Digital Democracy, told *Wired*.

Experimenting Without Consent

As Chester suggests, the teen research was not Facebook's first foray into psychometric research. A study published in 2014 revealed that Facebook had conducted a mass experiment on 689,003 unsuspecting users without their permission. The com-

Millions of Facebook users post personal details about who they are and what they like. Facebook allows its advertisers to target these users and post ads based on their interests.

pany randomly separated the users into two groups and then altered the users' news feeds, removing all of the positive posts from one group and all of the negative posts from the other. The company monitored the users' posts to see if the altered news feeds affected their moods. The researchers published the results in the *Proceedings of the National Academy of Sciences*. "When positive expressions were reduced, people produced fewer positive posts and more negative posts; when negative expressions were reduced, the opposite pattern occurred," stated the researchers. "These results indicate that emotions expressed by others on Facebook influence our own emotions, constituting experimental evidence for massive-scale contagion via social networks."[76]

Some people saw the experiment as an infringement on the privacy of the users. "It's a cool finding but manipulating unknowing users' emotional states to get there puts Facebook's big toe on that creepy line," wrote privacy reporter Kashmir Hill. "Ideally, Facebook would have a consent process for willing study participants: a box to check somewhere saying you're okay with being subjected to the occasional random psychological experiment that Facebook's data team cooks up in the name of science."[77]

Even when users agree to take part in a social media-sponsored survey, they cannot be sure exactly how the information they provide will be used. This became apparent in 2018 when Facebook's privacy problems once again became big news. A scandal broke revealing that British consulting firm Cambridge Analytica gained access to the personal data of 50 million Facebook users. The breach began with a researcher who made an online quiz. People who took the quiz exposed their own data as well as friends' data. Facebook had rules against selling or sharing data accessed this way, but the people involved ignored those rules. The data was used to create computer modeling that was used by the Trump campaign during the 2016 presidential race. Mark Zuckerberg, CEO of Facebook, publicly apologized for what happened even as members of Congress announced their intention to investigate the company's practices.

Violating Data Protection Laws

Some regulators have already taken action against Facebook's practices—specifically, those used for targeting users. In May 2017 privacy regulators in France, the Netherlands, Spain, Germany, and Belgium issued a joint statement condemning Facebook for violating their national privacy laws. France fined Facebook 150,000 euros ($164,000) for violating the country's data protection rules. After an investigation into the processing of the personal data of 9.6 million Facebook users in the Netherlands, the Dutch government's Data Protection Authority (DPA) found Facebook in violation of its nation's laws. "The company breaches Dutch data protection law including by giving users insufficient information about the use of their personal data,"[78] wrote the Dutch DPA. The Dutch regulators also found that Facebook uses sensitive personal data from users without their explicit consent. For example, the DPA found that the social networking company was using information about the sexual orientations of users in the targeting of ads—another violation of Dutch law. Facebook agreed to stop using sexual orientation data for advertising purposes, but the Dutch DPA said it would continue to monitor the situation, adding that if it found other violations, it would not hesitate to issue sanctions.

> "[Facebook] breaches Dutch data protection law including by giving users insufficient information about the use of their personal data."[78]
>
> —The Dutch Data Protection Authority

The French fine amounted to no more than a slap on the wrist to a company that reportedly earns more than $30 billion a year in targeted advertising worldwide. However, a new privacy law passed by the European Parliament will go into effect on May 25, 2018. The EU General Data Protection Regulation (GDPR) "was designed to harmonize data privacy laws across Europe, to protect and empower all EU citizens' data privacy and to reshape the way organizations across the region approach data privacy," states the GDPR website. The GDPR warns that noncomplying organizations "will face heavy fines."[79] David Martin, a senior legal officer at the European Consumer Organization, which would levy the fines, said that the fines could be as high as 20 million euros (US $24.3 million) or 4 percent of the company's global revenue, whichever is higher. In the case of Facebook, that could mean fines as high as $1.2 billion.

In the United States, the Federal Communications Commission (FCC) and the Federal Trade Commission (FTC) oversee electronic advertising and information gathering by private companies. In 2016 the acting FTC chairman, Maureen K. Ohlhausen, told the Eighth Annual Telecom Policy Conference that her agency had already brought "more than 150 privacy and data security enforcement actions, including actions against ISPs and against some of the biggest companies in the internet ecosystem."[80] For example, in 2017 the FTC announced that VIZIO, one of the world's largest manufacturers of Internet-connected televisions, agreed to pay a $2.2 million settlement. The company was accused of installing software on its televisions that invaded the privacy of 11 million homes, collecting viewing data without consumer knowledge or consent. "The FTC has generally been the lead privacy enforcer, and I think has been very aggressive at doing so," says Jules Polonetsky, a privacy expert and the CEO of the Future of Privacy Forum, a nonprofit organization that promotes responsible data collection. "At the end of the day, the willingness of the FCC and the FTC to use their authority effectively is what will determine whether the consumers are protected."[81]

SOURCE NOTES

Introduction: The Right to Be Left Alone

1. Quoted in Justia, "*Boyd v. United States*, 116 U.S. 616, 625 (1886)." https://supreme.justia.com.
2. Samuel D. Warren and Louis D. Brandeis, "The Right to Privacy," *Harvard Law Review*, December 15, 1890. http://groups.csail.mit.edu.
3. Warren and Brandeis, "The Right to Privacy."
4. Quoted in Michael Kassner, "Why Big Data and Privacy Are Often at Odds," TechRepublic, April 18, 2016. www.techrepublic.com.
5. Quoted in Jenni Ryall, "'We Don't Want a Police State': Edward Snowden Slams Australian Metadata Laws," Mashable, May 30, 2016. http://mashable.com.

Chapter 1: Government Spying

6. Quoted in Justia, "*Berger v. New York*, 388 U.S. 41 (1967)." https://supreme.justia.com.
7. Quoted in Justia, "*Katz v. United States*, 389 U.S. 347 (1967)." https://supreme.justia.com.
8. Quoted in Justia, "*Smith v. Maryland*, 442 U.S. 735 (1979)." https://supreme.justia.com.
9. US Supreme Court, *Timothy Ivory Carpenter v. United States*, oral arguments, November 29, 2017. www.supremecourt.gov.
10. US Supreme Court, *Timothy Ivory Carpenter v. United States*.
11. US Supreme Court, *Timothy Ivory Carpenter v. United States*.
12. US Supreme Court, *Timothy Ivory Carpenter v. United States*.
13. US Supreme Court, *Timothy Ivory Carpenter v. United States*.
14. American Civil Liberties Union, "E-mail Privacy." www.aclu.org.

15. Quoted in *SCOTUS Blog,* "Brief of Respondent Microsoft Corporation in Opposition Filed," *United States v. Microsoft Corporation*, August 28, 2017. www.scotusblog.com.
16. Quoted in Lawrence Hurley, "U.S. Supreme Court to Decide Major Microsoft Email Privacy Fight," Reuters, October 16, 2017. www.reuters.com.
17. Barton Gellman, Julie Tate, and Ashkan Soltani, "In NSA-Intercepted Data, Those Not Targeted Far Outnumber the Foreigners Who Are," *Washington Post*, July 5, 2014. www.washingtonpost.com.
18. Edward Snowden, "Snowden On: The Fourth Amendment," NBC News, May 29, 2014. www.nbcnews.com.
19. Rajesh De, "Remarks of Rajesh De, General Counsel, National Security Agency Georgetown Law School, February 27, 2013," National Security Agency, May 3, 2016. www.nsa.gov.
20. Dana Priest and William M. Arkin, "Top Secret America," *Washington Post*, July 19, 2010. www.washingtonpost.com.
21. Quoted in Dan Eggen and Dafna Linzer, "Judge Rules Against Wiretaps," *Washington Post*, August 18, 2006. www.washingtonpost.com.
22. Quoted in Charlie Savage, "Congress Approves Six-Year Extension of Surveillance Law," *New York Times*, January 18, 2018. www.nytimes.com.
23. Quoted in Savage, "Congress Approves Six-Year Extension of Surveillance Law."

Chapter 2: Corporate Prying

24. Quoted in Liam Quinn, "Two Academics Reveal How Twitter Told Them Donald Trump 'Dominated' the Campaign and Was a Lock to Beat Hillary," *Daily Mail* (London), December 25, 2016. www.dailymail.co.uk.
25. Quoted in Justia, "*United States v. Miller*, 425 U.S. 435 (1976)." https://supreme.justia.com.
26. US Supreme Court, *Timothy Ivory Carpenter v. United States*.
27. Cathy O'Neil, "The Era of Blind Faith in Big Data Must End," TED2017, April 2017. www.ted.com.
28. Quoted in Mona Chalabi, "Weapons of Math Destruction: Cathy O'Neil Adds Up the Damage of Algorithms," *Guardian* (Manchester, UK), October 27, 2016. www.theguardian.com.

29. President's Council of Advisors on Science and Technology, "Big Data: A Technological Perspective," May 2014. https://obamawhitehouse.archives.gov.
30. Quoted in Alyssa Provazza, "Artificial Intelligence Data Privacy Issues on the Rise," TechTarget, May 26, 2017. http://search mobilecomputing.techtarget.com.
31. Quoted in Provazza, "Artificial Intelligence Data Privacy Issues on the Rise."
32. Noah Apthorpe et al., "Spying on the Smart Home: Privacy Attacks and Defenses on Encrypted IoT Traffic," arXiv, Cornell University Library, August 16, 2017. https://arxiv.org.
33. Adam Clark Estes, "Don't Buy Anyone an Echo," Gizmodo, December 5, 2017. https://gizmodo.com.
34. Jay Stanley, "The Privacy Threat from Always-On Microphones like the Amazon Echo," *Free Future* (blog), American Civil Liberties Union, January 13, 2017. www.aclu.org.
35. Stanley, "The Privacy Threat from Always-On Microphones lke the Amazon Echo."
36. Quoted in US Supreme Court, *Timothy Ivory Carpenter v. United States*.
37. Quoted in Jared Newman, "Google's Schmidt Roasted for Privacy Comments," *PC World*, December 11, 2009. www.pcworld.com.
38. Quoted in Ryall, "'We Don't Want a Police State.'"

Chapter 3: Criminal Hacking

39. Quoted in Olga Kharif, "2016 Was a Record Year for Data Breaches," Bloomberg Technology, January 19, 2017. www.bloomberg.com.
40. Quoted in Duncan Riley, "Proposed Law Would Impose Huge Fines for Credit Reporting Agency Data Breaches," Silicon Angle, January 10, 2018. https://siliconangle.com.
41. Malwarebytes, "The New Mafia: Gangs and Vigilantes," December 11, 2017. www.malwarebytes.com.
42. Quoted in Dan Tynan, "The State of Cyber Security: We're All Screwed," *Guardian* (Manchester, UK), August 8, 2016. www.theguardian.com.
43. Jurijs Girtakovskis et al., *2017 Webroot Threat Report*. Broomfield, CO: Webroot, 2017, p. 13.

44. Cisco Systems, Inc., *Cisco 2017 Annual Cybersecurity Report*. San Jose, CA: Cisco Systems, 2017, p. 10.
45. Quoted in Ryan Francis, "Hospital Devices Left Vulnerable, Leave Patients at Risk," CIO, February 9, 2017. www.cio.com.
46. Quoted in AFP, "Cyber Kid Stuns Experts Showing Toys Can Be 'Weapons,'" SecurityWeek, May 16, 2017. www.security week.com.
47. Quoted in AFP, "Cyber Kid Stuns Experts Showing Toys Can Be 'Weapons.'"
48. Reuben Paul (@RAPst4r), "It was fun but I hope people did not miss the message—Secure IoT before the Internet of Toys becomes the Internet of Threats," Twitter, May 16, 2017, 3:14 a.m. https://twitter.com.
49. BBC, "Children's Messages in CloudPets Data Breach," February 28, 2017. www.bbc.com.
50. Quoted in Andrea Lucia, "North Texas Family's Nanny Cam Hacked," CBS DFW, August 11, 2016. http://dfw.cbslocal .com.
51. Quoted in Lucia, "North Texas Family's Nanny Cam Hacked."
52. Quoted in Jennifer O'Neill, "Family Discovers Hacked Images of Child's Crib Online," *Yahoo Parenting* (blog), April 7, 2015. www.yahoo.com.
53. Chris Duckett, "The IoT Security Doomsday Is Lurking, but We Cannot Talk About It Properly," ZDNet, October 30, 2016. www.zdnet.com.
54. Quoted in Danny Palmer, "175,000 IoT Cameras Can Be Remotely Hacked Thanks to Flaw, Says Security Researcher," ZDNet, July 31, 2017. www.zdnet.com.
55. Quoted in Stilgherrian, "Our Hackers, Who Art in Open Source, Deliver Us from Refrigerators," ZDNet, January 24, 2014. www.zdnet.com.
56. Hiawatha Bray, "Do Alexa and Other Such Devices Mean the End of Privacy?," *Boston Globe*, January 12, 2017. www .bostonglobe.com.
57. Bray, "Do Alexa and Other Such Devices Mean the End of Privacy?"
58. Quoted in Stilgherrian, "Our Hackers, Who Art in Open Source, Deliver Us from Refrigerators."

59. Quoted in Stephen Jewkes and Oleg Vukmanovic, "Suspected Russia-Backed Hackers Target Baltic Energy Networks," *Reuters*, May 11, 2017. www.reuters.com.

60. Quoted in Stilgherrian, "Our Hackers, Who Art in Open Source, Deliver Us from Refrigerators."

Chapter 4: Social Media Profiling

61. Quoted in Macy Bayern, "How AI Became Instagram's Weapon of Choice in the War on Cyberbullying," *TechRepublic*, August 14, 2017. www.techrepublic.com.

62. Quoted in Nichola Thompson, "Instagram Unleashes an AI System to Blast Away Nasty Comments," *Wired*, June 29, 2017. www.wired.com.

63. Quoted in Clover Hope, "Prude Instagram Censors Ban #Curvy from Search Results," *Jezebel* (blog), July 16, 2015. https://jezebel.com.

64. Quoted in Justia, "*Packingham v. North Carolina*, 582 U.S. (2017)." https://supreme.justia.com.

65. Quoted in Helena Horton and Alex Hudson, "Instagram Censors Photo of Fully-Clothed Woman Because She Is Menstruating," *Mirror* (London), March 26, 2015. www.mirror.co.uk.

66. Kashmir Hill, "Facebook Says It Did 'a Test' Last Year Using People's Locations to Make Friend Suggestions," Splinter News, June 28, 2016. https://splinternews.com.

67. Thomas Fox-Brewster, "Facebook Is Playing Games with Your Privacy and There's Nothing You Can Do About It," *Forbes*, June 29, 2016. www.forbes.com.

68. Theo Miller, "Facebook Proves Targeted Ads Are Worth Your Privacy," *Forbes*, August 9, 2017. www.forbes.com.

69. Facebook user, interview with the author, January 13, 2018.

70. Antonio Garcia-Martinez, "I'm an Ex-Facebook Exec: Don't Believe What They Tell You About Ads," *Guardian* (Manchester, UK), May 2, 2017. www.theguardian.com.

71. Quoted in Paul Armstrong, "Facebook Is Helping Brands Target Teens Who Feel 'Worthless,'" *Forbes*, May 1, 2017. www.forbes.com.

72. Quoted in Nitasha Tiku, "Get Ready for the Next Big Privacy Backlash Against Facebook," *Wired*, May 21, 2017. www.wired.com.

73. Quoted in Olivia Solon, "'This Oversteps a Boundary': Teenagers Perturbed by Facebook Surveillance," *Guardian* (Manchester, UK), May 2, 2017. www.theguardian.com.

74. Quoted in Tiku, "Get Ready for the Next Big Privacy Backlash Against Facebook."

75. Quoted in Tiku, "Get Ready for the Next Big Privacy Backlash Against Facebook."

76. Adam D.I. Kramer, Jamie E. Guillory, and Jeffrey T. Hancock, "Experimental Evidence of Massive-Scale Emotional Contagion Through Social Networks," *Proceedings of the National Academy of Sciences*, June 17, 2014. www.pnas.org.

77. Kashmir Hill, "Facebook Manipulated 689,003 Users' Emotions for Science," *Forbes*, June 28, 2014. www.forbes.com.

78. Autoriteit Persoonsgegevens et al., "Common Statement by the Contact Group of the Data Protection Authorities of the Netherlands, France, Spain, Hamburg, and Belgium," May 16, 2017. https://autoriteitpersoonsgegevens.nl.

79. European Union GDPR Portal, "Site Overview." www.eugdpr.org.

80. Maureen K. Ohlhausen, "Privacy Regulation in the Internet Ecosystem," Eighth Annual Telecom Policy Conference, March 23, 2016. www.ftc.gov.

81. Quoted in Alina Selyukh, "As Congress Repeals Internet Privacy Rules, Putting Your Options in Perspective," *All Tech Considered*, NPR, March 28, 2017. www.npr.org.

American Civil Liberties Union (ACLU)
125 Broad St., Eighteenth Floor
New York, NY 10004
www.aclu.org

Established in 1920, the ACLU is a nonpartisan, nonprofit organization with more than 2 million members, activists, and supporters. The organization works in courts, legislatures, and communities to defend individual rights and liberties guaranteed under the Constitution and the laws of the United States.

Center for Democracy & Technology (CDT)
1401 K St. NW, Suite 200
Washington, DC 20005
https://cdt.org

The CDT works to preserve the user-controlled nature of the Internet and champion freedom of expression. It supports laws, corporate policies, and technology tools that protect the privacy of Internet users and advocates for stronger legal controls on government surveillance.

Electronic Frontier Foundation (EFF)
815 Eddy St.
San Francisco, CA 94109
www.eff.org

Founded in 1990, the EFF works to ensure that the civil liberties guaranteed in the Constitution and the Bill of Rights are applied to cutting-edge communication technologies. The EFF enlists the help of lawyers, policy analysts, activists, and technologists to advocate on behalf of consumers, innovators, coders, and the general public.

Electronic Privacy Information Center (EPIC)
1718 Connecticut Ave. NW, Suite 200
Washington, DC 20009
www.epic.org

EPIC was established in 1994 to focus public attention on emerging privacy and civil liberties issues, including protecting democratic institutions, promoting algorithmic transparency, and defending the right to privacy. EPIC engages in a range of program activities, including policy research, public education, litigation, and advocacy.

Guardian Project
https://guardianproject.info

The Guardian Project creates easy-to-use secure apps, open-source software libraries, and customized mobile devices that can be used by anyone looking to protect his or her communications and personal data from unjust intrusion, interception, and monitoring. Its website contains links to its apps and online mobile security training.

Privacy International
62 Britton St.
London EC1M 5UY
United Kingdom
https://privacyinternational.org

Privacy International is a nonprofit organization that conducts investigations into surveillance practices and systems in countries across the world to inform debate. The organization advocates for good practices and strong laws to protect people and their rights.

FOR FURTHER RESEARCH

Books

Marc Goodman, *Future Crimes: Inside the Digital Underground and the Battle for Our Connected World*. New York: Anchor, 2016.

Nancy S. Lind and Erik Rankin, eds., *Privacy in the Digital Age: 21st-Century Challenges to the Fourth Amendment*. Santa Barbara, CA: Praeger, 2015.

Carla Mooney, *How the Internet Is Changing Society*. San Diego: ReferencePoint, 2016.

Cathy O'Neil, *Weapons of Math Destruction: How Big Data Increases Inequality and Threatens Democracy*. New York: Crown, 2016.

Roberto Simanowski, *Data Love: The Seduction and Betrayal of Digital Technologies*. New York: Columbia University Press, 2016.

Internet Sources

Mackenzie Adams, "Big Data and Individual Privacy in the Age of the Internet of Things," *Technology Innovation and Management Review*, April 2017. www.timreview.ca/article /1067.

American Civil Liberties Union, "Coalition Letter Urging Congress to Vote "No" on Reauthorization of Section 702 Surveillance Absent Significant Reforms," September 7, 2017. www.aclu.org/sites/default/files/field_document/2017-09 -07_coalition_letter_senate_vote_no_reauthorization _section_702_without_reform.pdf.

Clark D. Cunningham, "The Feds Can Read Your Email, and You'd Never Know," *New Republic*, September 22, 2016. https://new republic.com/article/137027/feds-can-read-email-youd-never -know.

Matt Ford, "Should Federal Prosecutors Be Able to Search Americans' Emails Overseas?," *Atlantic*, October 16, 2017. www.the atlantic.com/politics/archive/2017/10/microsoft-email-warrant -case/543027.

Gary Kasparov, "Pursuing Transparency and Accountability for Both Humans and Machines," *Avast Blog*, July 30, 2017. https:// blog.avast.com/pursuing-transparency-accountability-for -humans-and-machines.

Sanja Kelly, Madeline Earp, et al., "Freedom on the Net 2015: Privatizing Censorship, Eroding Privacy," Freedom House, October 2015. https://freedomhouse.org/report/freedom-net-2015 /freedom-net-2015-privatizing-censorship-eroding-privacy.

Sanja Kelly, Mai Truong, et al., "Freedom on the Net 2017: Manipulating Social Media to Undermine Democracy," Freedom House, November 2017. https://freedomhouse.org/sites/default /files/FOTN_2017_Final.pdf.

Michael Stelzner, "How Social Media Has Evolved and Where It Is Headed," SocialMedia Examiner, October 27, 2017. www.social mediaexaminer.com/how-social-media-has-evolved-and-where -it-is-headed-brian-solis.

INDEX

PICTURE CREDITS